rx 4/04

James Cook

and the Exploration
of the Pacific

Explorers of New Worlds

James Cook

and the Exploration
of the Pacific

Charles J. Shields

Chelsea House Publishers
Philadelphia

Prepared for Chelsea House Publishers by:
OTTN Publishing, Stockton, N.J.

CHELSEA HOUSE PUBLISHERS
Editor in Chief: Sally Cheney
Associate Editor in Chief: Kim Shinners
Production Manager: Pamela Loos
Art Director: Sara Davis
Director of Photography: Judy L. Hasday
Project Editors: LeeAnne Gelletly, Brian Baughan
Series Designer: Keith Trego

First Printing
1 3 5 7 9 8 6 4 2

Library of Congress Cataloging-in-Publication Data

Shields, Charles J., 1951-
    James Cook and the exploration of the
    Pacific / Charles J. Shields.
        p. cm. – (Explorers of new worlds)
Includes bibliographical references and index.
ISBN 0-7910-6422-0 (hc) – ISBN 0-7910-6423-9 (pbk.)
1. Cook, James, 1728-1779–Journeys–Juvenile literature.
2. Explorers–England–Biography–Juvenile literature.
3. Voyages around the world–Juvenile literature.
4. Oceania–Discovery and exploration–Juvenile
literature. [1. Cook, James, 1728-1779. 2. Explorers.
3. Voyages around the world.] I. Title. II. Series.

G420.C65 S55 2001
910'.92–dc21   2001028273

Contents

"Fish Come Alive as People"

This watercolor painting by an artist aboard one of Captain James Cook's ships shows the people of a Nootka village. The area Cook named Nootka Sound is located on Vancouver Island, which is north of the present-day state of Washington. Cook visited the area in 1778 while searching for a passage through North America from the Pacific Ocean to the Atlantic.

I

On a chilly spring day more than two centuries ago, the Nootka Indians on the Northwest coast of North America cautiously watched a strange sight. Two large "things" afloat on the water—for the Nootka had nothing to compare them to—entered the harbor near their village. Chief Maquinna, a serious-looking man with a frowning black mustache, sent his warriors in canoes to investigate.

The canoes paddled as close at they dared. From a safe distance, the warriors spied a man with a hooked nose, which reminded them of the profile of a dog salmon fish. Then they saw a second man with a bent back, making them think of the humpback salmon. On returning to shore, they reported that the strangers were "fish come alive as people."

Chief Maquinna remained skeptical. According to stories handed down through later generations of the Nootka, the chief ordered the warriors "to go out . . . and try to understand what these people wanted and what they are after."

This time, the canoes came closer. As they did, the strangers tossed them pieces of baked bread. The Nootka recognized this as a friendly gesture,

A wolf mask carved by a member of the Nootka tribe. These Native Americans lived on the Pacific coast of North America, in what today are the states of Oregon and Washington, and the Canadian province of British Columbia.

and decided that they should welcome these people. Seeing a man who seemed to be the strangers' leader, the warriors in the canoes began shouting, "Nootka, Itchme! Nootka, Itchme!" which means, "You go around the harbor!" They were eager to show off their accomplishments to the visitors.

It was a world-changing event, this meeting of two different peoples. But then, the leader of the strangers was a world-changer. His name was Captain James Cook. To him and the crews of the two British ships under his command—the *Resolution* and the *Discovery*—the date was March 30, 1778.

Cook was making his third voyage around the world. In an age when few human beings ventured very far from the place of their birth, Cook had landed on six continents. While scientists in Europe and colonial America were busy learning the secrets of electricity and bacteria in their laboratories, Cook had mastered the world's first ***chronometer***—a clock that enabled accurate ***navigation***. He declared that his goal was "not only to go farther than anyone had gone before but as far as possible for man to go."

On this journey to the coast of North America, he would try to answer a 150-year-old question—whether a passage existed through the continent that would link the Pacific Ocean with the Atlantic. He would find that there was no route which the ships of his day could use.

His contact with the Nootka would change their lives, too, as it turned out. Cook wrote in his journal, "A great many canoes filled with the Natives were about the ships all day, and a trade commenced betwixt us and them, which was carried on with the Strictest honesty on both sides. Their articles were the Skins of various animals, such as Bears, Wolves, Foxes, Deer, Raccoons, Polecats, Martins and in particular the Sea Beaver [otter]."

When Cook's ships reached Macao in Indochina the following year, merchants eagerly purchased the fur pelts for thousands of dollars. Soon, European trappers and traders would arrive hungering for more, forever ending the isolation of the Northwest Indians from the rest of the world.

Still another remarkable discovery lay before Cook–his last one. After leaving the Northwest, Cook would sail south into the heart of the Pacific Ocean and discover the Hawaiian Islands. Thousands of cheering native people would charge the beaches at the sight of his ships, joyously welcoming their arrival, and honoring Cook as a god.

But that was a year away. For now, Cook and his men enjoyed their interaction with the Nootka. As the canoes approached, one of the paddlers sang one long note of greeting, and then the others picked it up.

The Nootka then sang their best songs, which the sailors applauded. Then the sailors returned the favor, calling up the fife and drum players to play something lively. One of Cook's lieutenants remarked on the Nootka's unusually respectful reaction: "these were the only people we had seen that ever paid the smallest attention to those or any of our musical Instruments, if we except the drum, & that only I suppose from its noise & resemblance to their own drums; they observed the profoundest silence."

One of Cook's crew members wrote, "The halloo is a single note in which they all join, swelling it out in the middle and letting the sound die away. In a calm with the hills around us, it had an effect infinitely superior to what might be imagined from any thing so simple."

That night, as many as 10 to 12 canoes continued to circle the *Resolution* and *Discovery*. The Nootka were very curious about the British ships.

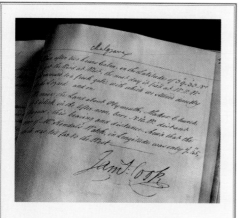

Captain Cook noted every important event in his journal. Each night, on large pieces of paper and mostly in pencil, he summed up the day in plain style. After Cook's voyages the journals were published, allowing the British public to enjoy his adventures. Cook showed himself to be a thoughtful observer not only of geography, but also of people and their customs.

During the next several days, the trading continued, and the British permitted the canoe-riders to come aboard. But then trouble started. The natives thought that everything their new friends had was meant to be shared. They began helping themselves to iron nails, wooden handles, bags of fishhooks, and even a small anchor. Cook complained in his journal, "They made no scruple of stealing when the opportunity offered; but upon being detected they would immediately return whatever they had taken and laugh in our faces."

Cook could not tolerate their stealing, even if he understood that "they considered it as a piece of Dexterity that did them credit rather than dishonor." As an officer of the British navy, and a man whose strictness was well-known, theft violated his sense of order. As an individual who had succeeded all his life through discipline and self-sacrifice, it went against the grain of his character. When his gold watch disappeared from his cabin (it was returned) the officers formally went on the alert against the Nootka's "thievish tricks."

Over such an incident in Hawaii, and his stern reaction to it, Captain James Cook would lose his life, ending one of the most extraordinary stories in the history of exploration.

This painting of Captain James Cook was made by a man who sailed with him, John Webber. Cook was the second eldest of eight children; however, only three of his siblings survived childhood.

Cook's Early Life

2

$\mathcal{J}$ ames Cook's early life seems an unlikely start for someone who would later become famous as a ship's captain and explorer. In fact, the home he grew up in had no connections to the sea or the British navy at all.

Cook was born in the village of Marton-in-Cleveland in the Yorkshire countryside of England on October 27, 1728. His father James, a Scottish farm laborer, had married a Yorkshire girl named Grace Pace. James senior seems to have believed that hard work would bring rewards. He rose to the position of farm **overseer** and could afford to move his family into a nicer home. From Marton, the family moved to the nearby village of Great Ayton, where they lived in a small stone cottage beside a stream.

Young James was able to attend a nearby school, where he showed a gift for mathematics. However, in those days not even a basic education could greatly change the lives of most people. Cook worked as a farm laborer, just as his father had. When he was 17 he agreed to work for William Sanderson, the owner of a general store in the harbor town of Staithes. Friends and family probably thought Cook's talent with numbers suited him for business.

For a year and a half, Cook learned the trade of running a shop as an *apprentice*. But his life in Staithes—a town tucked away at the foot of a cliff with only one steep road leading out of it—left him restless. The duties of a shop-boy filled the long hours of the day. At night, he slept under the counter. Whenever he found time to himself, he sat on the docks, watching the boats come and go.

Some historians believe Cook eventually ran away. But this behavior seems out of character for him. A more believable story is that Mr. Sanderson recognized his apprentice's unhappiness and they ended the arrangement in a friendly way.

When James Cook was eight, his family moved to this stone farmhouse in Great Ayton, England.

Cook packed his few belongings, took the road that led up over the cliff, and walked the 13 miles to the bustling port of Whitby. Then he stood on the dock and offered his services to the first merchant ship that would take him. Within a short time, Cook shipped out as a deckhand on the *Freelove.* This vessel mainly carried coal from Newcastle to London. But it is certain the ship visited Ireland, Norway, and the Baltic Sea, too.

Work aboard ***colliers***–coal-carrying ships– turned out to be the right choice for Cook. He gained good experience, and took to the life of a seaman very well. So well, in fact, that he was promoted to mate in 1752. This put him in line to command his own ship. During the winters, Cook spent his time ashore studying mathematics.

The Seven Years' War, which started in 1756, was a struggle that pitted Prussia (an area of Europe that is part of modern-day Germany) and England against Austria, France, and Russia. England had already been at war with France for about 150 years; a battle for control of North America had started two years earlier, in 1754. This became known as the French and Indian War. Both conflicts ended in 1763.

But then in 1755, a year before the Seven Years' War began, Cook joined the British navy. By now he was 27, and boys as young as 14 held higher rank than he did. But Cook's experience gave him an edge over other sailors. Within a month of duty aboard the 60-gun *Eagle*, Cook was promoted to **boatswain**. Two years later, he sailed as master of his own ship, the *Solebay*.

In October 1757, Cook became master of the much larger *Pembroke*, a 64-gun warship. When the *Pembroke* was sent to North America to assist a British attack on the French-held city of Quebec, the admiral of the British fleet gave Cook a dangerous assignment: chart the channel of the St. Lawrence River right up to the French lines. At night, Cook sailed a small boat close to the enemy, taking note of the water's depth, currents, and the outline of the shore. One night, Indians surprised him by leaping on the stern of his boat. He dove off the bow and swam for his life. Finally, his mission complete, he produced navigational charts that were used to guide the successful British assault on Quebec.

When the war ended in 1763, Cook was given additional surveying assignments. As skipper of the schooner *Grenville*, he spent several summers making maps of the eastern coasts of Canada. He then returned to the St. Lawrence aboard the *Pembroke* and conducted a better survey of the river.

So far, Cook's career in the British navy had been brilliant. He had been promoted from enlisted man to ship commander in ten years. This was very unusual for a farm boy without connections to the top decision-makers in the navy. His success rested on two personal traits: a willingness to teach himself what he needed to know, and a strong sense of duty.

Cook had made one powerful friend, however,

in Sir Hugh Palliser, the governor of Newfoundland during the summers Cook mapped the Canadian coast. Palliser befriended and encouraged Cook. It was probably Palliser who set Cook on the path to the South Pacific.

In 1766, the government was searching for someone to lead an extraordinary scientific expedition. It involved a prediction made by Edmund Halley, a famous **astronomer**. In 1716, Halley had predicted that on June 3, 1769, the planet Venus would pass in front of the sun (the next time this would occur would not be until 1874). When this happened, scientists figured, the distance from the sun to the Earth could be calculated by measuring the time it took Venus to cross the face of the sun. To ensure a good view of this rare event, the Royal Society, a group of England's brightest scientists, urged that special telescopes be set up at three locations: northern Norway, Hudson Bay in upper Canada, and the island of Tahiti in the South Pacific.

Almost immediately, bickering erupted over who would have command of the ship carrying the scientists to the South Pacific. The competition attracted some famous names determined to have the honor. The leading geographer in Britain, for

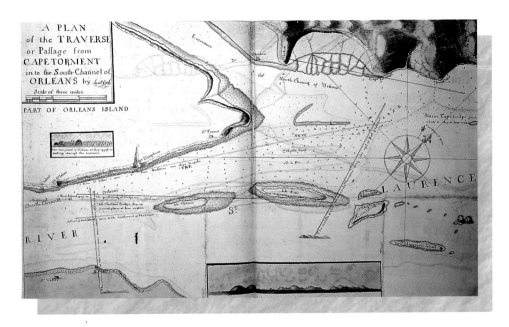

This is one of Cook's maps of the St. Lawrence River.
His drawings and figures were so reliable that they
remained in use until the early 20th century.

example, Augustus Dalrymple, insisted that he must have control over the whole expedition. The British navy, charged with supplying a good ship, said no.

Then the Royal Society proposed a candidate who was not famous or widely educated, but who came highly recommended, most likely by his friend Hugh Palliser: 39-year-old Captain James Cook. The government and the British Admiralty agreed on the choice. In 1768, Cook officially received the appointment, opening the door to the first of his three historic voyages.

Cook's Endeavour *sets sail for the South Pacific. Before being refitted for the voyage, the* Endeavour *had been a collier similar to the ships on which Cook began his seafaring career. Like other colliers, it was sturdy, built with thick timbers, and flat-bottomed for sailing into shallow harbors.*

The Endeavour 3

o some leading thinkers in London, the choice of Cook for command of the South Pacific expedition made no sense. After all, men such as Commodore John Byron or Captain Samuel Wallis, both **aristocrats**, had already led voyages to the Pacific Ocean. James Cook, on the other hand, came from the working class.

In the view of the British navy, however, Cook had already shown the right qualities for this undertaking. He had sailed the rugged coast of Canada, carefully mapping its bays and inlets. Also, because the waters of the South Pacific were unfamiliar, the navy preferred a man of

Cook's military background to give the orders. His training could make the difference between success or failure. Finally, his reports would add details and descriptions to the usual information. Cook had a sharp eye for picking out what was new or strange, a skill the members of the Royal Society appreciated. Who better to identify the hundreds of locations the ship would visit, many of them never before seen by Europeans?

On April 3, 1768, a grimy collier called the *Earl of Pembroke* arrived at the naval shipyard on the Thames River near London. The ship had been chosen for the upcoming mission—perhaps at Cook's suggestion. A collier could hold the large amounts of supplies and scientific equipment the voyagers would need. At 106 feet long and almost 30 feet wide in the middle, it was not a graceful craft, but it was strong and it could sail in only 14 feet of water—perfect for entering shallow tropical harbors.

For four weeks, carpenters worked on the ship, which was renamed the *Endeavour*. Its hull and masts were repaired, and new sails and **rigging** were hauled into place. For defense against attacks, workers mounted 12 small cannons on swivels bolted to the deck. On May 18, the former coal carrier was

Captain Cook's Personal Life

There can be no doubt that the trust placed in Cook added polish to his naval career. But one can only guess what effect his responsibilities had on his personal life. In 1762, Cook had married Elizabeth Batts. During their 17 years of marriage, she would only see him every few years, and then only for short periods of time. When Cook took command of the *Endeavour*, he had two small boys at home–five-year-old James and four-year-old Nathaniel. His daughter Elizabeth was less than a year old and Mrs. Cook was expecting a fourth child.

On August 26, 1768–the day his son Joseph was born–Captain Cook sailed from Plymouth, England, aboard the *Endeavour* for the South Pacific. Three weeks later, baby Joseph died. Three months before Cook returned to England in 1771, tiny Elizabeth died as well. The Cooks had six children in all. Only James lived into adulthood, but he drowned at sea at 31. However, Captain Cook never wrote a word about any of these personal misfortunes. The journals he kept during his three voyages contain nothing about his life outside the navy.

ready. The *Endeavour* anchored in the river beside the mighty warships of the British navy, ready for its new commander, James Cook.

The ship's handpicked crew numbered about 80–most of them young sailors eager for adventure. The 11 scientists chosen to go included **botanist** Joseph Banks, ***naturalist*** Daniel Solander, astronomer Charles Green, and artist Sydney Parkinson, who planned to draw plants and animals unfamiliar to European eyes.

The *Endeavour* sailed first to the Madeira Islands

Joseph Banks was only 25 years old when the Endeavour *left England, yet he already had a growing reputation as a botanist. The presence of scientists such as Banks on Cook's voyages reflects the importance placed on scientific discovery during the 18th century.*

in the Atlantic Ocean off the northwest coast of Africa. Then in November the ship reached the white beaches of Rio de Janeiro on the coast of Brazil. However, Portuguese officials kept the vessel inside the harbor for two months. They suspected the former coal-carrier might be a pirate ship. By January

Cook received two sets of instructions. The first explained what needed to be done so the scientists could view Venus from Tahiti. The second were secret orders—not to be opened until the scientific work on the island was complete.

1769, the *Endeavour* finally continued on its way to Cape Horn at the tip of South America, rounding it safely into the Pacific Ocean with no trouble from the wind or weather.

During a long voyage such as this one, life aboard ship was hard. Normally only officers enjoyed any privacy. But the *Endeavour* offered even less room than most ships because of its special mission. Food, supplies, and scientific equipment crowded the space below deck. A second problem facing the crew—as on all long voyages—was *scurvy*. This is a disease caused by lack of vitamin C, which is found in such foods as citrus fruits, tomatoes, lettuce, celery, onions, carrots, and potatoes. Sailors with scurvy suffered from sore joints, poor appetite, bleeding gums, and loose teeth.

Cook's men ate the fare of most 18th century sailors. They added fresh fish that they caught to their main diet of salted meat, cheese, biscuits, and rum. A goat on board provided fresh milk. Sometimes, to celebrate special events, the sailors drank wine and slaughtered one of the pigs kept in a pen.

More than most captains of the day, however, Cook took extra steps to safeguard the health of his crews. He insisted that his men eat such foods as onions and sauerkraut. In addition, he ordered them to bathe regularly, exercise, clean their clothing, and air out their bedding. Cook believed these measures would prevent scurvy and poor health. His sailors grumbled, but the number of deaths on Cook's ships ran far below the average in the British navy.

Once the ship turned under South America and sailed into the Pacific, the

The British navy would eventually adopt Cook's methods to keep its sailors healthy. In 1795, the navy began to issue lime juice to its crews to help prevent scurvy. This led to a nickname for British sailors: "limey."

This is the main cabin in a replica of Cook's ship. There was not much room aboard the Endeavour—*it was only about a tenth the size of the* Pembroke, *the warship Cook had commanded in Canada.*

Endeavour headed north toward Tahiti, stopping at small islands to replenish fresh water or food now and then. On April 11, 1769, the lookout on the top-mast spotted their destination.

For the next two days, the crew struggled to get the ship safely into the island's Matavai Bay. They had arrived seven weeks before Venus would pass in front of the sun. But after eight months at sea, the crew felt no regret about being in beautiful Tahiti for almost two months with practically nothing to do.

Tahiti and
the Secret
Orders

Captain Cook and several of his officers meet with a group of Pacific islanders. In Tahiti the natives and the visiting English sailors were able to live comfortably side by side.

4

he Tahitians cautiously greeted Cook and his men. They were becoming used to the sudden arrival of white strangers.

The first European to visit Tahiti had been the British sea captain Samuel Wallis in 1767. He claimed the island for Britain. The next year, a French navigator named Louis-Antoine de Bougainville arrived at Tahiti and claimed it for France. (Generally, the empire-building nations of the 16th through the 19th centuries refused to admit that "discovered" land already belonged to the peoples living there, especially if the natives seemed uncivilized to them.) Now here was another ship of visitors. But the Tahitians warmed up when they recognized one of Cook's lieutenants who had served under Captain Wallis.

For the next few months, the crew and islanders settled into a comfortable living arrangement. The Tahitians had a very open society, with little importance placed on ownership of property. Cook had to order his men not to take advantage of them, but for their part, the sailors complained of being robbed and pickpocketed by the natives. Cook stressed the importance of being friendly. When the captain met King Oree of the neighboring island of Huaheine, he wisely agreed to trade names, making himself "Oree" and the king "Cookee."

But then a crisis arose—some islanders stole an important piece of the observatory. Cook warned the chief about the seriousness of this crime. After all, the whole reason for the voyage was to observe Venus crossing the sun. A search party chased the thieves to the other side of the island and forced them to surrender the equipment. But it had been

A color view of one of the South Pacific islands where the Endeavour *dropped anchor shows several types of native crafts. This painting was made by artist William Hodges, a member of several of Cook's voyages.*

taken apart, and lay in pieces. Fortunately, Joseph Banks reassembled it in time for the important astronomical event on June 3.

In addition to astronomer Charles Green, Cook, Banks, and other members of the crew observed the transit of Venus. Unfortunately, no one could agree on the exact amount of time it took for the planet to cross the sun. Observers at the sites in Norway and Newfoundland faced the same problem. Ultimately, the information collected was practically useless.

With this part of the mission finally finished,

This 1570 map of the world depicts a large southern continent that many geographers thought existed. Belief in this continent, called Terra Australis Incognita, lasted until Cook's voyages in the late 18th century.

Cook opened the second set of instructions from the Royal Society–the secret orders given to him in England. He read that his mission was to provide an answer to a long-asked question: Does the mystery continent shown on maps as Terra Australis Incognita ("Unknown Land of Australia") really exist, or is there only ocean in the unexplored part of the Southern Hemisphere?

The geographer Augustus Dalrymple had spent ten years trying to answer this question. According to his figures, the total known area of the Earth's land and its oceans did not equal the Earth's size. Therefore an undiscovered continent must exist somewhere in the South Pacific. The British government was also eager to find this continent, because a vast unclaimed land area meant an opportunity to expand its empire.

Personally, Cook did not believe a word of it. The currents on the way to Tahiti hinted at no large land mass nearby. But his orders were clear. He was to proceed southward as far as the 40th latitude. If he did not find land on this course, then he was to turn west and search between latitudes 40 and 35. If still more ocean lay ahead, he should continue on until he reached the eastern side of the land already discovered by the Dutch navigator Abel Janszoon Tasman in 1642. (Tasman had discovered New Zealand, and later explored a section of the coast of Australia. Geographers hoped Tasman's **landfall** formed a piece of a huge continent.)

After Tahiti was mapped, Cook prepared to leave. Two islanders volunteered to go along: Tupaia, a local chief and priest, and his servant.

On August 9, 1769, the expedition shoved off from Tahiti. Tupaia offered prayers for fair winds to help the ship. A few days later, Cook found he was in the middle of dozens of islands, at least 75, lying close together. He named them the Society Islands and claimed them for Britain.

The *Endeavour* sailed on in a southerly direction through the South Pacific. Cook steered to 40 degrees latitude, where the geographers at the Royal Society expected a continent. But no sign of land poked above the horizon. The weather turned sour. Cook turned northward and continued west. At the end of September, pieces of floating seaweed appeared on the water and seabirds squawked overhead, meaning land was near. On October 7, a 12-year-old ship's boy, Nicholas Young, sighted the eastern side of New Zealand's North Island.

Two days later, Cook anchored in what he later named Poverty Bay because he couldn't find the supplies he needed. The large bump of land at one end of the bay he named Young Nick's Head. Going ashore, he found the soil good and the trees gorgeous. He commented that the land was excellent for settlement "should this ever be thought an object worth the attention of Englishmen."

The people living there—the fiercely tattooed Maori—were **cannibals**. Cook's crew soon met them in the bay. The Tahitian priest Tupaia could speak with them, and told Cook they were unfriendly. Defiantly, a Maori stole the sword of one of Cook's officers. A crewman shot him dead.

The *Endeavour* turned south to explore the coastline. They met with more hostility, however. Somehow, Tupaia's servant fell into the hands of natives, who took off with him in a canoe. Cook's men fired at the paddlers, killing two or three. The boy jumped out and swam back to the ship. Cook named the southern tip of the bay Cape Kidnappers.

Cook wanted to prove that New Zealand was an island, not part of a larger continent. He sailed the *Endeavour* closely along the coast until the ship returned to Poverty Bay again in mid-March. Once the scientists and officers agreed with the captain's assessment, the *Endeavour* turned homeward. With fresh supplies aboard, the ship left New Zealand.

On April 20, 1770, Cook reached the unexplored east coast of Australia. Sighting it, the ship turned north and Cook claimed 2,000 miles of coastline for Great Britain. On April 29, the ship entered a bay, which Cook first named Stingray Bay. But Joseph

Banks and the other scientists discovered huge numbers of unknown plant specimens, so the captain renamed it Botany Bay. As the English explored the area, two **Aborigines** fired darts at the strangers. Banks feared the darts might be poisoned. Cook calmly scared off the attackers with musket fire.

The distance to England was still far and the *Endeavour* began to show the scars of two years of sailing: a leaking hull, weakened masts, rotten rigging, and torn sails. Cook passed between Australia and New Guinea—proving these lands were not one continent—and put into Batavia, a Dutch port in Indonesia (now called Jakarta), for repairs.

It was a mistake, but he had no choice. Forced to stay until December until the ship's repairs were finished, the crew fell ill with **malaria** and **dysentery**. Not one man had been lost to scurvy during the journey from England to Batavia, but now they died one after another. The first to die was the ship's surgeon, William Monkhouse. The Tahitian Tupaia and his servant soon followed. Eventually most of the crew, including Cook and Banks, were sick and weak. By the time the *Endeavour* set out for Cape Town, South Africa, on the day after Christmas, seven men had died. Twenty-two more succumbed

Captain Cook lands in Botany Bay, Australia, in April 1770. By 1788, Botany Bay would become the unhappy destination of convicts deported from England.

to disease during the voyage, including the the astronomer Green and artist Parkinson. Four more men died at Cape Town. After the ship left port and headed toward England, two officers died. One of these was Cook's top lieutenant, who had been suffering from tuberculosis for a long time. "He hath been dieing ever since, tho he held out tollerable well until we got to Batavia," Cook wrote sadly.

On July 13, 1771, Nicholas Young sighted Land's End, England, and the *Endeavour* wearily dropped anchor that same day. The voyage had lasted for nearly three years.

The Voyage to
the Bottom
of the World

Explorers of New Worlds

This painting by James Clevely, a carpenter on Cook's voyages, shows the British ships anchored at one of the Society Islands. Only a year after Cook's first voyage to the South Pacific ended, he was setting out again. This time, his orders were to sail south to determine once and for all whether a large continent existed there.

5

he Royal Society, the navy, the newspapers—all hailed Cook's first voyage as a solid success. (The newspapers, however, called it "Banks' voyage.")

Cook had not discovered a new continent. Nor had he discovered Tahiti, Australia, or New Zealand—they were already known to Europeans. But Cook's thoroughness in exploring the South Pacific added tremendously to the knowledge about the world's geography. His journal brimmed with descriptions of winds and currents, reefs and barriers, people and the lands they lived in. More than just serving as the skipper of a ship that carried scientists around the world, Cook took on the role of explorer-geographer.

Apart from his scientific achievements, the navy also recognized Cook's feats as a navigator. He had plotted incredibly straight and true courses across great distances. Cook was promoted as a reward.

But a question remained: could a continent exist even farther south of the waters in which Cook had sailed? The government wanted this question settled once and for all. In the autumn of 1771, a few months after Cook returned home to his family, he received a new assignment: search the bottom of the world for a continent. The government promised to provide two ships.

Cook quickly arranged for two colliers like the *Endeavour* to be hauled into dry dock and refitted. The *Resolution*, Cook's **flagship**, was 111 feet in length and 35 feet wide in the middle for the 110 crewmen and scientists aboard. The *Adventure* was 97 feet long and would carry 80 crewmen and scientists. Tobias Furneaux, a distinguished officer, would command the *Adventure*.

For some reason, Joseph Banks expected this trip to be more comfortable. He invited friends along, telling them they would travel in style. While the ships were in dry dock, Banks ordered special quarters to be built for his private group on the main deck of the *Resolution.* However, the added rooms made the ship top-heavy and difficult to sail, and Cook ordered them torn down. Banks stormed off in a rage. He eventually decided not to go on the voyage.

What happened to the *Endeavour*? The ship may have met its end in 1778, during the American Revolution. It is believed that rather than let the Americans capture the vessel, the British sank it in 25 feet of water in Newport Harbor, Rhode Island. The hull of a ship thought to be the *Endeavour* was recently discovered at the bottom of the harbor.

Cook's instructions were to travel south to Cape Circumcision and find out if it was part of a larger continent. If so, he was to take possession in the name of the king of Britain. If it was not part of a continent, then he was to sail as far south as possible and *circumnavigate* the area, looking for a way in. When the ice and weather proved too harsh, he could turn north again.

On this voyage, Cook would have the advantage of navigating with a new instrument called the chronometer—a sea clock. Before Cook's day, fixing a ship's position was guesswork. To find a ship's position, a navigator needed to know the exact time in order to read tables of stars' positions accurately. But with only a sand hourglass aboard, the navigator depended on rough estimates. In 1735, inventor John Harrison, an English jeweler, made a clock that would keep perfect time under the conditions at sea. This allowed more precise navigation. Cook called his chronometer, "my trusty friend the watch."

At 6 A.M. on July 13, 1772, the *Resolution* and the *Adventure* departed Plymouth, England. Heading

The chronometer invented in 1735 by John Harrison revolutionized navigation. Cook took four chronometers with him on his second voyage, two on each ship. As a result, he was one of the first ship's commanders able to chart his exact position.

due south, they reached Cape Town, South Africa, 109 days later. On November 23, 1772, Cook sailed south from Cape Town toward unknown waters.

Thirteen days later, a lookout on the *Adventure* called out "Land!" But what he had mistaken for land turned out to be an iceberg. The ships sailed on. On January 17, 1773, they crossed the Antarctic Circle. For two months they followed the edge of an endless ice pack, looking for a passage, rolling and pitching in the freezing water and dodging the merciless icebergs. The rigging on the ships sagged with icicles. Yet conditions would grow worse—winter was still on its way to the Southern Hemisphere.

When the ships were well south of the area in which previous discoveries had been reported, Cook decided to turn north. On March 25, after sailing some 10,600 miles through uncharted waters, the *Resolution* and *Adventure* put into Dusky Bay, New Zealand. Cook then spent a few months exploring the islands of the South Pacific.

On November 27, the ships turned south again. Two months later, they reached the unyielding ice pack and could go no further. Powerful winds blew tall mountains of ice—some as high as 60 feet— toward the ships. Fog increased the chances of a collision. Cook wrote that the ice "extended east and west far beyond the reach of our sight, while the southern half of the horizon was illuminated by rays of light which were reflected from the ice to a considerable height. . . . It was indeed my opinion that this ice extends quite to the Pole, or perhaps joins to some land to which it has been fixed since creation."

Cook once again wintered in New Zealand, leaving in November 1774 for his third try. But a gale separated the *Resolution* and the *Adventure* shortly afterward. The *Adventure* returned to New Zealand. When Captain Furneaux sent a party of men ashore to gather supplies, Maori cannibals overpowered and killed them. Disheartened, Furneaux ordered the *Adventure* to sail for England alone.

Cook, meanwhile, sailed across the South Pacific and arrived five weeks later at Tierra del Fuego, in South America. After a short rest, the ship continued on into the South Atlantic. Then suddenly, land appeared. This discovery caused great excitement—had they finally found the edge of a southern continent? It turned out to be an island covered in ice, which Cook named South Georgia.

Resisting a temptation to turn north toward home, Cook continued to sail south. At the end of

Cook sailed closer to the South Pole than any man had before him. The ice-filled waters forced him to turn back before he and his men could see Antarctica.

January he sighted a group of islands even more desolate than South Georgia. Cook named these the South Sandwich Islands for the Earl of Sandwich, the Lord of the Admiralty. After spending a week exploring them, he finally turned north for England, reaching England on July 30, 1775.

The voyage had lasted three years and eight days and had covered more than 60,000 miles. Cook lost only four men—just one to illness, and none to scurvy. And he had proved there was no southern continent near the bottom of the world, unless it was at the Pole itself.

Cook's Final Voyage

Explorers of New Worlds

Captain Cook, at left, is surrounded by angry Hawaiian islanders in this painting attributed to John Cleveley. His brother James Cleveley was a ship's carpenter who witnessed the death of Cook on February 14, 1779.

6

ord of the hardships faced by Cook and his men quickly spread. For his extraordinary efforts to sail beyond icebergs to the southern end of the earth, the Royal Society awarded him a gold medal. In addition, the Society made him a *fellow* of the organization, honoring him as a man of science. The navy promoted him to post-captain and offered him a desk job at the Greenwich Hospital, which would provide him a comfortable income for life.

The only sour note was the mishandling of his journal from the first voyage. When Cook read what a scholar had done to his **manuscript**, he threatened to withdraw his name from the book.

The dispute involved a difference in writing styles. Cook's publisher had hired a man named John Hawkesworth to rewrite the journals in the popular fancy language of the time. For example, when Cook said he walked with the king of the island, Hawkesworth changed it to "the commander pursued his journey under the auspices of the potentate." Cook was shocked by the dishonesty. He knew he could not write this way with his education.

The publisher eventually gave the manuscript to a clergyman named John Douglas to edit. Douglas mainly left Cook's writing alone, except to correct his horrible spelling and to add some footnotes of explanation.

When the book, titled *A Voyage Towards the South Pole and Round the World,* was published in May 1777, it became very popular. The first printing sold out in a day. Soon more copies were printed. A French translation of the book was also published.

At age 46, Cook could look forward to retiring in style from his post at the Greenwich Hospital. But he also expressed his willingness to serve his country if needed. He did not have to wait long.

Following the gale during the second voyage that separated the *Adventure* from the *Resolution,* Captain Furneaux had stopped at Tahiti. There he took aboard a native who wished to see England. After the Tahitian had visited England, the Admiralty ordered Captain Charles Clerke to return the man home as an act of goodwill. This errand grew into another voyage—to find the Northwest Passage.

During the previous two centuries, many explorers had attempted to find a passage from the Atlantic Ocean to the Pacific Ocean through North America. If European nations could reach the Pacific without having to sail around the tip of South America, their trading and military power would increase enormously.

But every attempt at probing for a passage had come from the Atlantic Ocean side. The Admiralty determined that Clerke's trip to the south Pacific provided an excuse and an opportunity to try a different approach. Why not enter the Pacific through the Indian Ocean on the west and look for a Northwest Passage along the uncharted northwestern coast of North America?

The Admiralty consulted Cook on the details. He volunteered not only to help organize the voyage but to take command of it as well. The *Adventure* was unseaworthy, so Cook turned once again to the fleet of North Sea colliers. He chose a ship to be refitted and renamed the *Discovery*. Clerke took the helm of the *Discovery* and its crew of 70, while Cook settled into the captain's quarters of the *Resolution* again with its crew of 112.

On July 12, 1776–almost exactly one year since returning from his second voyage–Cook left on his third and, as it turned out, final voyage of discovery.

The *Discovery* and *Resolution* rounded the Cape of Good Hope, sailed through the Indian Ocean and headed for landfalls Cook knew well by now–New Zealand, Tahiti, and other Pacific islands. Turning north, in January 1778 he became the first known European to sight some of the smaller Hawaiian islands. But the mission was to search for the Northwest Passage, and so they continued on.

In March, the mainland of North America appeared on the horizon. The friendly Nootka Indians greeted them, introducing them to beautiful pelts that would later set off a scramble for trade and trapping in the Northwest. All summer the British

The Resolution *and* Discovery *swing at anchor in a bay on Eimeo, one of the Society Islands. This painting was done by John Cleveley during Cook's third voyage.*

ships explored the coast from Oregon northwards, rounding the tip of the Alaska **Peninsula**, through the Bering Strait, and into the Arctic Ocean. There, Cook and his men endured many of the same hardships they had experienced in the Antarctic Circle–cold, storms, and icebergs. There was no sign of an ice-free passage into the continent.

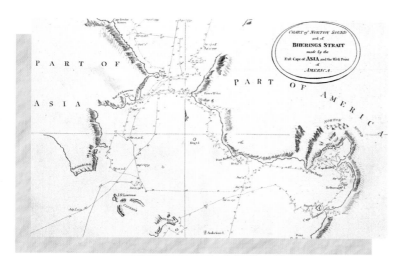

Cook's chart of the Bering Strait, made during his exploration of the Pacific Coast of North America during the summer of 1778. Cook paid close attention to detail and was careful in recording his ships' positions each day. As a result, his maps were very accurate.

Cook turned south to replenish and repair the ships for the next year. Remembering the pleasant appearance of the Hawaiian islands, he headed for the main island. Upon reaching it, the ships entered Kealakekua Bay on the Kona coast and dropped anchor.

The former farm laborer from Yorkshire was about to be hailed as a god. The Hawaiians were celebrating the start of the season of their god Lono makua. In a solemn ceremony, they walked around the island, bearing banners of white cloth hung on crosspieces–looking much like masts with sails. To the natives' astonishment, the white strangers in the bay seemed to be flying the same banners. When Cook stepped ashore, the overwhelmed islanders wrapped him in red cloth. The chiefs escorted him to religious sites. At first Cook was bewildered, but he quickly realized how the natives had misunderstood the situation.

For the next two months, the Hawaiians devoted themselves to entertaining close to 200 English sailors and scientists. The effort was expensive. Cook may have made a mistake in allowing himself and his men to be treated as gods. In any case, the halos around the crews gradually dimmed as fights broke out between the English and the natives. The Hawaiians suspected something was wrong when one of the "immortals" from the ships died and was buried on the island.

With relief, the islanders bid the men good-bye in early February. The *Discovery* and *Resolution* headed north to continue looking for a passage.

But within a week, the ships returned. A storm had broken one of the *Resolution*'s masts, and Cook put in for repairs. This time the Hawaiians were not happy to see their former guests. Perhaps out of anger, or maybe just for the chance to steal some iron, a native took off with one of the ship's boats.

This was exactly the type of behavior Cook would not tolerate. The summer before, the Nootka had been a nuisance by robbing his ships. Cook resorted to a method he had used before. With nine armed **marines**, he came ashore on February 14, 1779. Cook demanded that Chief Kalei'opu'u come with him as a **hostage** until the boat was returned. Normally, this maneuver was harmless, as Cook remained on good terms with native people. But this time, the Hawaiians' patience had run out.

As Kalei'opu'u accompanied Cook to the beach, his wife rushed to him, pleading with him not to go. Two other chiefs then argued with Kalei'opu'u. The chief listened and changed his mind–he wouldn't go after all. A crowd of islanders surged toward Cook's men, armed with spears and rocks.

Suddenly, down the beach, a Hawaiian tried to paddle away in a canoe. A marine jerked his musket to his shoulder, fired, and killed him. Shouts filled the air. Cook attempted to reach his boat but the mob blocked his way. He drew a two-barreled pistol and fired once. The buckshot bounced off the hardened coconut war shield of a man he was aiming at.

He fired again and killed a Hawaiian.

As the crowd rushed the soldiers, Cook's men fired but had no time to reload. Cook waded into the surf and signaled to his ship for help. A blow to his head from a war club pitched him forward, but not before he was stabbed and speared from behind. The marines who managed to escape to the ship reported that four of the landing party had been killed, in addition to Captain Cook.

Later, the ships' officers negotiated for the return of their captain's body, which the Hawaiians agreed to do. Cook's remains were buried at sea. After the funeral, the *Resolution* and *Discovery* made another try at finding the Northwest Passage, but they were unsuccessful and returned home in October 1780.

Cook had vowed "not only to go farther than anyone had done before but as far as possible for man to go." He had done exactly that by reaching the ends of the earth. In addition, he had applied scientific findings to exploration, demonstrated the value of the chronometer in accurate navigation, raised the standards of health and cleanliness on ships that had been plagued by disease, and opened the mysterious and vast Pacific Ocean to future exploration, settlement, and scientific investigation.

Chronology

1728 James Cook is born October 27 in the village of Marton-in-Cleveland in the Yorkshire countryside of England.

1746 Begins working as a sailor for a coal shipping company owned by Henry and John Walker.

1752 Is promoted to mate in the collier fleet based in Whitby, England.

1755 Joins the British navy a year before the Seven Years' War breaks out.

1759 Charts the St. Lawrence River in preparation for a successful English attack on the French fort at Quebec.

1762 Marries Elizabeth Batts of Shadwell, England.

1763 Service during the war earns him praise and additional assignments exploring and mapping the coast of Canada.

1768 Receives appointment from the Royal Society to command a scientific voyage to the South Pacific; *Earl of Pembroke*, a coal ship, is renamed *Endeavour* and selected to serve as Cook's ship; on August 26, sails from Plymouth, England, to begin first voyage to the South Pacific.

1769 The *Endeavour* arrives in Tahiti on April 13; the passage of Venus across the sun is observed in June; Cook lands in New Zealand in October.

1770 Reaches the unexplored east coast of Australia on April 20, and claims it for Great Britain.

1771 *Endeavour* arrives back in England on July 13; in the fall Cook receives a new assignment—to search for a continent near the South Pole.

1772 *Resolution* and *Adventure* depart Plymouth on July 13 to begin Cook's second global voyage.

1773 Cook and his sailors become the first men to sail deep into the Antarctic Circle on January 17.

1774 The English explore the Society Islands, Easter Island, the Marquesas, New Hebrides, and New Caledonia; *Adventure* returns to England.

1775 *Resolution* arrives in England on July 30.

1776 On July 12, *Resolution* and *Discovery* leave England to begin Cook's third and final global voyage, this time to find the Northwest Passage.

1777 *Resolution* and *Discovery* visit New Zealand, the Society Islands, and other islands in the South Pacific; Cook's book *A Voyage Towards the South Pole and Round the World* is published in May and becomes an immediate best-seller.

1778 In January, Cook's ships sight the Hawaiian islands, which were previously unknown to Europeans; in March, Cook reaches the coast of Oregon; during the summer, charts the Alaskan and Canadian coastline while searching for the Northwest Passage; sails south for the winter and reaches Hawaii at the end of November.

1779 After leaving Hawaii on February 4, the *Resolution*'s mast is damaged in a storm; Cook returns to Hawaii, where he is killed in a dispute with the islanders on February 14.

1780 The *Resolution* and *Discovery* return to England in October.

Glossary

Aborigine—a name for a native person of Australia.

apprentice—someone who works for a person who is skilled in a trade or craft, in exchange for learning from that person.

aristocrat—a member of the highest or noble class.

astronomer—a person who studies the stars, planets, and other objects in the sky.

boatswain—the member of a ship's crew who is responsible for taking care of the ship's hull.

botanist—a person who studies plants.

cannibals—humans who eat the flesh of other humans.

chronometer—an instrument for measuring time with great accuracy.

circumnavigate—to sail completely around.

collier—a large, broad-bottomed ship used to carry coal.

dysentery—a disease, usually caused by infection, in which patients lose blood and have severe diarrhea.

fellow—a member of a scientific or literary society.

flagship—the ship that carries the commander of a fleet and displays his flag.

hostage—a person held captive by one group of people to ensure that promises will be kept or demands will be met by another group.

landfall—the land first sighted on a voyage.

malaria—a disease of the blood, transmitted by mosquitoes, that causes severe chills and fever and can be deadly.

manuscript—a written work before it is published.

marines—soldiers who serve on board a ship, or in close association with a naval force.

naturalist—a person who studies the natural development over a period of time of plants and animals in a specific region.

navigation—the science of directing the course of a seagoing vessel, and of determining its position.

overseer—a person who supervises the work of others.

peninsula—an area of land surrounded by water on three sides, with the fourth side connected to a larger body of land.

rigging—the lines and chains used aboard a ship to raise and lower the sails and support the masts and spars.

scurvy—a disease caused by a lack of vitamin C, which was once common on long sea voyages. Its signs include spongy gums and loose teeth, soreness in the arm and leg joints, and bleeding into the skin and mucous membranes.

Further Reading

Beaglehole, John C. *The Life of Captain James Cook*. Stanford, Calif.: Stanford University Press, 1992.

Frost, Alan. *The Voyage of the Endeavour: Captain Cook and the Discovery of the Pacific*. London: Allen and Unwin, 1998.

Haney, David. *Captain James Cook and the Explorers of the Pacific*. New York: Chelsea House Publishers, 1992.

Hough, Richard. *Captain James Cook*. New York: W. W. Norton, 1997.

Robson, John. *Captain Cook's World: Maps of the Life and Voyages of James Cook R.N.* Seattle: University of Washington Press, 2000.

Stefoff, Rebecca. *Scientific Explorers: Travels in Search of Knowledge*. New York: Oxford University Press, 1993.

Suthren, Victor. *To Go upon Discovery: James Cook and Canada, 1758-1767*. London: Dumdum Press Ltd., 1999.

Withey, Lynne. *Voyages of Discovery: Captain Cook and the Exploration of the Pacific*. New York: William Morrow and Company, 1987.

Picture Credits

CHARLES J. SHIELDS lives in Homewood, a suburb of Chicago, with his wife Guadalupe, an elementary school principal. He has a degree in history from the University of Illinois in Urbana-Champaign, and was chairman of the English department and the guidance department at Homewood-Flossmoor High School in Flossmoor, Illinois.